RANGERS – FOOTBALL LEGE
1873-1973

Compiled by
Stuart Marshall

The Song of the Good Old Rangers F.C.

Tune—"Ye Mariners of England."

Ye followers of Rangers,
Who cheer the Old Light Blues,
Who back the fine old Ibroxites
To win, and never lose.
You mind the days of bold Nick Smith,
Neil Gibson, Donald Gow.
McPherson, Drummond, Dickie, who
Once showed all others how.

CHORUS.

They were beat, clean and neat,
By the hardy old Light Blues,
'Twas a treat, quite complete,
Just to see the Old Light Blues,
And the battle never raged for long
Till the other side had changed their song
When the Rangers laid them low,
When the Rangers laid them low.

Ye followers of Rangers,
Who watch their game to-day,
Whose hearts beat fast, when Alec. Smith
And Bennett romp away.
When Galt, and good old Billy Hogg,
Keep the ball upon the roll,
Till they cross it on to Willy Reid
Who bangs it into goal.

CHORUS.

R. F. Morrison.

No. 2259—Copyright.

FOREWORD

The match against Real Madrid at Ibrox in the 1963 European Cup was my first visit to see the Light Blues. Unfortunately, due to no small measure by Puskas and DiStefano, the 1-0 score was not in our favour. I was fortunate to witness not only the emergence of, to me, the greatest Ranger ever, 'Slim Jim' Baxter, but also Henderson, Johnston, Greig, McKinnon, Wilson and Jim Forrest. You may wonder why I mention the latter, but if so, look up his scoring record (sorry Ally!). There are many stories I could relate but the one I like best is when John Greig's wife was supposedly phoned to be told he had broken a leg: 'Who's?' was her reply.

However, the book is not about me or just the '60s; it looks at a 100 year period when newspapers, comics, packets of cigarettes or sweeties gave away photos or cards of the football legends of the era. In the early days boys badgered men at street corners with the plea, 'Got any fag cards, mister?' Now grown men, like me, who have been collecting this stuff for twenty years or more pay sometimes large sums of money for the give-aways of yesteryear. Why do we do this? Because we're Rangers fans! And in my case a Bully Wee fanatic.

The Scottish Cup Final Team, 1876-1877. Rangers lost 3-2 to Vale of Leven, but it took a second replay before they were beaten.

Back row: George Gillespie, William McNeil, Tom Vallance, J.M. Watt.
Middle row: William Dunlop, David Hill, Peter Campbell, Moses McNeil, Sam Ricketts.
Front row: James Watson, A. Marshall.

Rangers had a humble beginning. A band of working lads clubbed together for a ball and started to play on the Flesher's Haugh. They then decided to call themselves the Rangers Association Football Club. What is less well known is that Rangers were named after an English Rugby Union club, having been chosen by Moses McNeil whose brother Peter was Rangers' first ever captain in their inauguration into the Scottish Cup in 1874. The year 1873 saw the birth of the club. From Flesher's Haugh they eventually, via Glasgow Green and Burnbank, arrived at Kinning Park where they remained for a few years before taking up residence at Ibrox Park in 1877. Not until the 1890s did Rangers start to establish themselves as a team of class. Then they defeated their bitter rivals, later to be known as the other half of the Old Firm, four times in succession. In 1885-86, they refused to play the English team Rawtenstall in the English Football Association because the opposition had professionals in their team.

The story of Rangers from the early days when they shared a pitch with the Great Eastern team, through to the present day with their magnificent stadium, could be likened to the story of Scottish Football during the past 100 years and their domination of the Scottish game is still as unassailable today as it was all those years ago.

Sir John Ure Primrose, Lord Provost of Glasgow and chairman of the club from 1912 to 1923.

On 8 September, 1888, Rangers played a Canadian touring team in a one all draw. This was one of the club's worst ever seasons and of the 39 matches played, nineteen were lost and seven drawn with 93 goals for and 108 against. The tide however was turning and the following season they began a reconstruction process that is still going on to this day.

"Should auld acquaintance be forgot."

"And the days of Auld Langsyne."

TOM VALLANCE
Requests the Presence of
Mr J. S. McKenzie
TO SUPPER
IN THE
METROPOLITAN
40 HUTCHISON ST.
on the occasion of the
21ST ANNIVERSARY
OF THE
FINAL CUP TIE
PLAYED
13TH APRIL 1877.

SCOTTISH CUP

TOM VALLANCE CAPTAIN

Vale of Leven Team,
1876-77.
Wm. C. Wood.
Archibald Michie.
Andrew M'Intyre.
William Jamieson.
Alexander M'Lintock.
John Ferguson.
David Lindsay.
John M'Dougall.
Robert Paton.
John C. M'Gregor.
John C. Baird.

Rangers Team.
Thomas Vallance.
George Gillespie.
Wm. B. M'Neil.
Sam. Ricketts.
David Hill.
James Watson.
Moses M'Neil.
J. S. MacKenzie.

J. FERGUSON CAPTAIN

IN MEMORIAM
Alex. Marshall.
P. M. Campbell.
W. Dunlop.
J. Watt.

WEDNESDAY, 13TH APRIL, 1898.

The invitation card to the 21st Anniversary dinner celebrating the club's victory over Vale of Leven. Tom Vallance was team captain for nine years and president from 1883 to 1889.

Back row: H. McCreadie, J. Steel, N. Smith, D. Haddow, D. Mitchell.
Middle row: A. McCreadie, D. Boyd, W. Wilson (secretary), J. Drummond, J. MacPherson, J. Barker.
Front row: R. Marshall, the Scottish Cup, the Glasgow Cup, J. Gray.

The first Rangers team to lift the Scottish Cup, 1894. The final was played at Old Hampden (later to become Cathkin Park, home to Third Lanark) and saw Celtic beaten 3-1. In the same year Rangers beat Cowlairs 1-0 to lift the Glasgow Cup, a magnificent looking trophy.

Little material from Rangers' first twenty years is available to the collector. J. Baines of Bradford and Barnsley sold cards in packets through from 1880 until 1920. They came in a variety of shapes such as diamonds, hearts, rectangles, fans and balls and were usually in full colour. All are very rare and only about ten different Rangers cards are known to exist. Pears Soap gave away similar cards and these are even rarer.

Back row: A. Robb, P. McLaren, A. Barr, Sam Bryson.
Middle row: P. Rennie, A. Binnie, G. Lyon, J. Yuille, D. Chisholm, J. Greig, D.M. McLeod.
Front row: D. Barclay, J. McNeish, J.M. McLean (Secretary), J. McDonald, W. Prentice.

The Rangers' XI of 1896 when the team still played played in junior competitions. Ten years earlier the Scottish Junior Association agreed that the 3rd XIs of senior clubs could be admitted to Junior competition as long as no individual player had taken part in any senior cup ties, hence the above team would have been Rangers' third team.

Back row: T. Low, M. Dickie, N. Smith, J. Miller, J. Muir (Committee), T. Hyslop, A. Smith, J. Oswald, R. Neil, J. Drommond (inset).
Front row: J. MacPherson, N. Gibson, D. Mitchell, A. McCreadie, T. Turnbull.

The Glasgow Cup, Scottish Cup and Glasgow charity cup are lined up in front.

1896-97 was one of Rangers' greatest ever seasons. The football played that year was described as brilliant by those who saw it and while only finishing third in the league they won all three cups that season.

Robertson.
Glasgow Rangers.

Ogden's Cigarettes.

R. C. McColl.

OGDEN'S CIGARETTES

D Series.

PACKETS OF

OGDEN'S
TAB
CIGARETTES

Contain Photos. of
GENERAL INTEREST.

R. C. Hamilton, Scotch
International,
Rangers F.C., Glasgow.

This Series contains
200 Photographs.

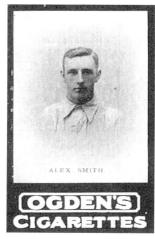

ALEX. SMITH.

OGDEN'S CIGARETTES

R. C. HAMILTON.

OGDEN'S CIGARETTES

R. C. Hamilton

OGDEN'S CIGARETTES

Ogdens issued these cards, known as 'Tabs', with packets of their Tab cigarettes between 1899 and 1904. There was a sports series and a general interest series and quite a few Rangers players appear. Some players feature on more than one card and two of the general interest series show the match in progress on the day of the 1902 Ibrox Disaster. R.C. McColl is misnamed – he is actually R.S., the man who later started the newsagent chain.

JACK ROBERTSON

OGDEN'S CIGARETTES

Back row: J. Wilson (Trainer), J. Henderson (President), N. Smith, D. Crawford, N. Gibson, M. Dickie, J. Stark, R. Neil,
J. Robertson, J. Drummond, W. Wilson (Match Secretary), A. Mackenzie (Committee).
Front row: J. Campbell, J. Graham, J. MacPherson, R.C. Hamilton (Captain), F. Speedie, A. Sharp, A. Smith.
Inset: J. Miller, D. Mitchell, J. Wilkie, T. Hyslop.

When will we see their likes again – the League Champions, 1898-99. Played eighteen, won eighteen, lost nil, drawn nil. Enough said.

A. SMITH,
Glasgow Rangers.

J. CAMPBELL,
Glasgow Rangers.

F.& J. Smith, the Glasgow cigarette manufacturers who later became part of Imperial Tobacco, issued this set of 120 'Footballers' (usually referred to as 'Smith's Brown Backs') in early 1900. All of these players played for Scotland with J. Campbell achieving the distinction of gaining seven caps (international and inter-city) all in the year 1899.

N. SMITH,
Glasgow Rangers.

M. DICKIE,
Glasgow Rangers.

D. CRAWFORD,
Glasgow Rangers.

N. GIBSON,
Glasgow Rangers.

J. McPHERSON,
Glasgow Rangers.

The pictures on these early postcards, both autographed by the players, are from cigarette cards. Robertson's is one of the 'Brown Backs' while Smith's is from a series of thirty 'Footballers' issued by J.&F. Bell of Glasgow. J.T. Robertson was an Everton player when he was capped against England in 1898 and was at Southampton when capped again against England the following year. A Dumbarton lad, nicknamed 'Jacky', he joined Rangers in August 1899. One of the all time greats, he was capped another twenty times after joining the Ibrox team. Although a half-back, he was almost as a good a forward and occasionally played outside-right or centre forward.

Shortly before joining Rangers in 1894, Alex Smith played in the Ayrshire Junior Cup, helping Darvel Juniors to success. An outside-left, Alex played all his senior career with Rangers (except for one match for Kilmarnock against Sunderland), lasting 21 seasons and winning 34 caps for Scotland in both full and league internationals.

A match played during the 1907-08 season. On the facing page are players from the team who played in the match. Rangers are in the dark strip but it is difficult to say who their opponents were.

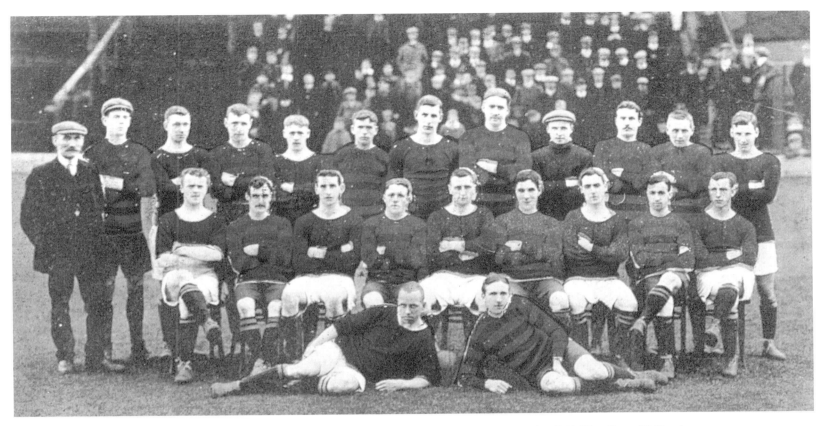

Back row: J. Wilson (Trainer), G. Livingston, A. Barrie, J. MacDonald, J.T. Butler, R.C. Hamilton, J.J. Dunlop, A. Newbigging, J. Spiers, G. Law, J. Gordon.
Middle row: A. Craig, J. Bell, J. Galt, J. Dickie, R.G. Campbell, J. Currie, A. Kyle, G.R. Watson, A. Smith.
Front row: J. May, W. Henry.

1907-08 was not a good season for the club as they were beaten four times by their Old Firm rivals, twice in the league and once each in the Scottish Cup and the Glasgow Cup.

F.&J. Smith's 1908 'Footballers'. The set of 100 cards runs from 2 to 104 (numbers 1, 13, 53 and 54 were unissued). This set is often referred to us the 'cup-tie' set. On the left is a thin paper advert, probably an insert in a newspaper, found by a workman who uncovered it behind an old fireplace.

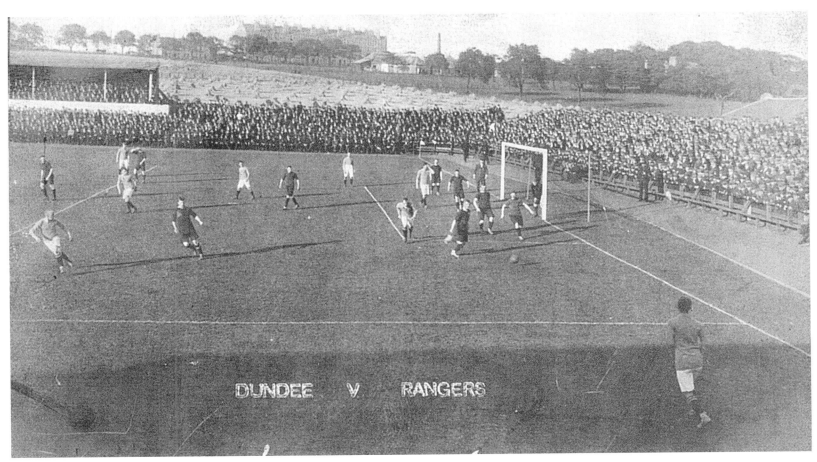

A match, *c.* 1910; from the hay bales gathered behind the ground, it looks likely that it was played around August or September. Postcards of matches are extremely rare – I suppose this was because the players couldn't stand still long enough for a good photograph to be taken.

Back row: W. Yuille, J. McLean, J. Stark, R.G. Campbell, J. Galt, J. Gordon, J. may, W. Hunter.
Middle row: H. Rennie, G. Waddell, W. Reid, T. Gilchrist, G. Law, A. Thomson, W. McPherson, H. Lock.
Front row: J. Wilson (Trainer), A. Bennett, T. Miller, W. Hogg, J. Mackenzie, A. Craig, J. Jackson, A. Smith.

This is one of fifteen postcards I possess of different Scottish teams, given out with the magazine *Ideas* around 1910. I suspect that there were sixteen in the set and that the missing one may be Queen's Park – can anyone help me complete my collection?

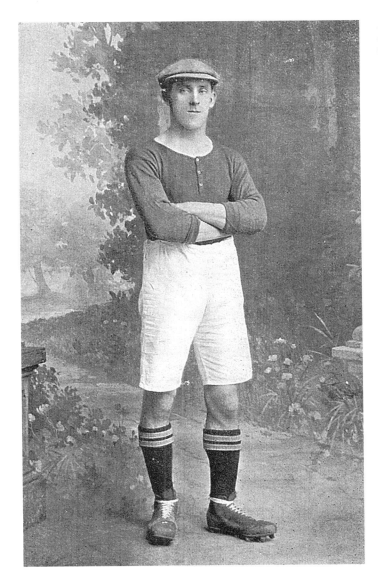

Left: English by birth, H. Lock came to Rangers from Southampton where he had established a great goalkeeping reputation. This postcard was issued around 1910.

Right: In March 1905 Alec Craig, a left back, arrived at Ibrox from Rutherglen Glencairn. A few days later he was picked for the injury decimated Rangers team in their semi-final Scottish Cup match against Celtic. It was a rough match and eventually it had to be abandoned due to trouble in the crowd. The match was ultimately conceded to Rangers, allowing them into the final only to be beaten by Third Lanark.

Back row: J. Wilson (trainer), G. Ormond, G. Chapman, R.G. Campbell, J. Galt, W. Hogg, J. Cameron, W. Reid, A. Richmond, A. Gibson, G. Law.
Middle row: A. Bodin, J. Gordon, G. Waddell, J. Bowie, H. Lock, A. Bennett, R. Parker, A. Smith.
Front row: R. Brown, J. Paterson, J. Goodwin, A. Brown, J. Hendry.

1911-12 was the year that Clyde, the 'Bully Wee', knocked Rangers out of both the Scottish Cup and the Glasgow Charity Cup. In the Scottish Cup, Clyde were leading 3-1 when, with fifteen minutes to go, the pitch was invaded and the game abandoned. Rangers decided to retire from the competition rather than ask for a replay. They compensated by winning both the League and the Glasgow Cup by beating Partick Thistle in the final.

R.G. CAMPBELL
GLASGOW RANGERS F.C.

A. SMITH
GLASGOW RANGERS F.C.

SERIES OF 150
No 28
FOOTBALLERS

WM. HOGG.

A burly and speedy Englishman, and one of the dangerous men in the "Light Blue" attack. He requires a lot of stopping when in motion and centres beautifully and can score goals from the most difficult positions.

SMITH'S
ALBION GOLD FLAKE
CIGARETTES

W. REID
GLASGOW RANGERS F.C.

J. GALT
GLASGOW RANGERS F.C.

J. BOWIE
GLASGOW RANGERS F.C

'Footballers', a series of 150 cards issued in 1912. Several printings were made and these can be found in varying shades of blue or black. The text can vary and there are minor design changes between printings, with keylines appearing or disappearing.

J. GORDON
GLASGOW RANGERS F.C.

Only very recently did I acquire this postcard – I wonder where No. 1 and No. 2 are. Southend is on the Kintyre Peninsula and the card was produced by C.F. Roger of Argyle Studios, Campbeltown. £50 was the price put on the card by a dealer but what price the team? On the facing page is the same team ready for action.

Back row: Riddell, Hendry, Paterson, Robertson.
Middle row: J. Wilson (Trainer), Montgomery, Ormond, Campbell, Farrington, Hogg, Ferguson, Galt, Lawrie, Gordon.
Sitting: Boden, Reid, R. Brown, Bowie, Lock, Bennett, Parker, Smith.
Front row: A. Brown, Goodwin.

A very elusive postcard, *c.* 1912.

J. PATERSON,
Rangers F.C.

J. GALT,
Rangers F.C.

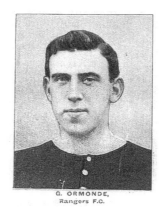

G. ORMONDE,
Rangers F.C.

J. BOWIE,
Rangers F.C.

J. GORDON,
Rangers F.C.

The *Glasgow Weekly Mail* series of 'Famous Footballers of 1913-14', issued in sheets of nine portraits were given away with each issue of the paper over eleven weeks. Each sheet featured a different category, e.g. 'Scotland's Favourite Left Half-Backs'. The 'Right Backs' and 'Goalkeepers' did not contain any Rangers players.

J. L. LOGAN,
Rangers F.C.

ALEX. SMITH,
Rangers F.C.

WILLIAM REID,
Rangers F.C.

A. BENNETT,
Rangers F.C.

Back row: A. Cunningham, J. Smith, G. McQueen, D. Meiklejohn, H. Lawson, J. Sutherland, T. McDonald, G. McMillan, T. Cairns.
Middle row: G. Livingston (Trainer), J. Walls, T. Reid, H. Lock, R. Manderson, W. Robb, H. McKenna, A. Archibald.
Front row: A. Laird, A. Dixon, G. Henderson, J. Bowie, J. Low, T. Muirhead, A. Johnston, A.L. Morton.

This plain-backed postcard was found along with various other cards of Scottish teams but nobody seems to know how they were distributed. Can you help? The 1920-21 team played 42 league games, winning 35, drawing six and losing only one. The single defeat was by Celtic on New Year's Day 1921 when many of the regulars were missing due to injuries.

Back row: J. Nicholson, J.R. Smith, T. Cairns, W. Robb, D. Meiklejohn, H. Johnston, A. Dixon.
Front row: A. Archibald, W. McCandless, T. Muirhead, R. Manderson, A. Cunningham, G. Henderson, A. Morton.

Distributed with the *Pluck* comic on 2 December 1922, this card was No. 6 of a series of 27 'Famous Football Teams'.

Back row: McDonald, Reid, Kirkwood, Walls, Kilpatrick, Ireland, Rollo, Roberts, McCandless.
Middle row: Hamilton, Meiklejohn, Jamieson, Craig, Nicholson, Henderson, Johnston, Dixon, Lawson, Robb.
Front row: Archibald, Muirhead, Cairns, Manderson (Captain), Cunningham, Morton, Hansen.

This card was printed on thick paper in sepia-gravure and has a plain back. It was distributed in the comic *Pals* in 1923 and is quite an elusive card.

TRIBUTE TO

GOOD OLD SANDY ARCHIBALD

The Flying Fifer o' the Glesca Rangers F.C.

Tune—"*Sandy yer a Dandy*"

There's a player wha fairly tak's the e'e,
A guid yin noo ye'll a' agree;
On the ba' he's a treat tae see—
    O' Sandy, he's a dandy.
The wey that he can dance aboot,
And bangs the ba' wi' either foot,
   Nae wonder the spectators shout—
    O' Sandy, yer a dandy!

CHORUS.

O' Sandy, yer a dandy,
  O' Sandy, yer a don,
Ye come in awfu' handy
  As the goals yer pilin' on.
Wi' yer tricky little touches
  As guid as e'er we saw.
We've had ootside richts in Scotland,
  But yer the dandy o' them a'.

Fifteen years ye've been a Ranger noo,
And donned the colours bonnie blue,
And aye proved sae staunch and true—
    O' Sandy, yer a dandy.
Tae see ye prancin' doon the wing
And get the ba' on the swing,
Mony a braw goal it does bring—
    O' Sandy, yer a dandy.

Union St.,   R. McLeod.
Cowdenbeath.

A. ARCHIBALD, Rangers.

Sandy Archibald joined Rangers in May 1917 and became an Ibrox hero over seventeen seasons, playing 666 matches and scoring an incredible 162 goals. Sandy helped to win thirteen league championships, the Scottish Cup three times, and the Glasgow Cup and the Charity Cup ten times each. The postcard on the left was produced in Fife while the picture on the right featured in the *Adventure Album of the Cup Fighters of 1925*.

Back row: Purdon, Hodge, Smith, Asborne, Moyies, Hamilton, McGregor, Manderson, Fleming, McKay.
Middle row: Chalmers, Hamilton, Archibald, Craig, Ireland, Kirkwood, Shaw, Henderson, Cunningham, Weir.
Front row: William Struthers, Meiklejohn, Gray, Morton, Dixon, Muirhead, Marshall, G.T. Livingston (Trainer).
(One of the players in the front row was not named on the original postcard.)

This card was distributed with *The Citizen*, a paper that labelled itself 'the Green Un' – the Footballer's Favourite'.

Back row: R. McPhail, W. Hair, H. Shaw, W. Moyies, A. Cunningham, R. Hamilton.
Middle row: D. Meiklejohn, T. Lockie, J. Marshall, R. Ireland, T. Craig, J. Docherty, A. Archibald, J. Hamilton, J. Fleming, J. Simpson, D. Gray, J. Osborne, T, Hamilton.
Front row: W. McCandless, G. McMillan, T. Muirhead, W. Chalmers, A.L. Morton.

The squad, 1927-28. Twenty-five years had passed since Rangers had last won the Scottish Cup but on 14 April 1928, 120,000 spectators packed Hampden to watch them take on their Old Firm rivals. It was a tight game and the result rested on a solitary incident when Willie McStay of Celtic handled the ball, conceding a penalty. As captain, David Meiklejohn elected to take the kick and as he recalled, 'If I scored we would win; if I failed, we would be beaten. It was a moment of agony.' He scored and Rangers went from strength to strength. They finally won 4-0 and a hoodoo was laid to rest. The team that day was T. Hamilton, R. Hamilton, Gray, Buchanan, Meiklejohn, Craig, Archibald, Cunningham, Fleming, McPhail and Morton.

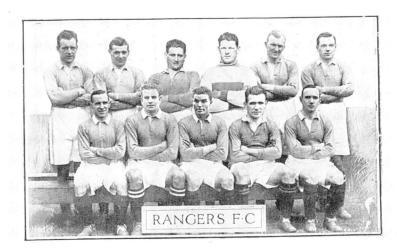

Back row: Meiklejohn, Archibald, Gray, T. Hamilton,
Cunningham, McPhail.
Front row: Morton, Fleming, R. Hamilton, Craig, Muirhead.

Back row: Archibald, Fleming, Meiklejohn, T. Hamilton,
Cunningham, R. Hamilton, Buchanan.
Front row: W. Struth (Manager), Gray, Craig, Muirhead (Captain),
McPhail, Morton, J. Kerr (Trainer).

Right
Back row: Muirhead, R. Hamilton, Archibald, T. Hamilton,
Cunningham, Meiklejohn.
Front row: McPhail, Gray, Fleming, Craig, Morton.

These postcards were amongst a variety given away with McEwan's Ale.
Dating from between 1928 and 1930, they were distributed in large numbers
but few survive today. The card I like best is the one autographed by the
legendary Bob McPhail.

Back row: Fleming, Marshall, R. Hamilton, Morton, McDonald, T. Hamilton, Brown, McCandless, Buchanan.
Front row: McPhail, Archibald, Gray, Meiklejohn, Muirhead, Craig.

This photograph was stapled into postcard-sized booklets containing five other teams: Dundee, Partick Thistle, Queen's Park, Falkirk and Celtic. The booklets were given away by James Aitken & Co. who ran a brewery in Falkirk.

Back row: J. Kerr (Trainer), D. Meiklejohn, J. Marshall, A. Archibald, J. Fleming, T. Hamilton, J. Buchanan, T. Craig, W. Struth (Manager).
Front row: G. Brown, D. Gray, R. McDonald, T. Muirhead (Captain), R. McPhail, R. Hamilton, W.G. Nicholson, A.L. Morton.

In the 1929-30 season, Rangers won everything, including the League Championship, three senior cups, the Second Eleven Cup and the Scottish Alliance Championship. The achievement was by no means easy and in fact the Charity Cup was won on the toss of the coin, captain Meiklejohn calling 'heads' correctly when Celtic captain James McStay threw up the penny. Both the finals of the Scottish Cup (Partick Thistle beaten 2-1) and the Glasgow Cup (Celtic thrashed 4-0) were won on replays after 0-0 draws in the first games. This photograph was used by the *Hotspur* comic in 1961, No. 6 in a set of twelve 'Famous Teams in Football History'.

Back row: T. Hamilton, J. Fleming, J. Buchanan, S. English, M. Hailstones, G. Brown, R. Main, R. McAuley, J. Dawson.
Middle row: W. Struth (Manager), R. Hamilton, J. Marshall, J. Smith, R. McPhail, W.R. Deans, A. Archibald, J. Simpson, W. Nicholson.
Front row: G. Conlin, R. McDonald, J. Murray, D. Meiklejohn (Captain), R. McGowan, D. Gray, T. Craig, A. Morton, J. Kerr (Trainer).

This plain-backed card of the 1931-32 team was distributed by an unknown periodical of the time. This season saw the club crash back to earth as, having won the league five times in a row, they had to settle for second place. However, they did take the Scottish Cup, beating Kilmarnock 3-0, the Glasgow Cup (beating Queens' Park 3-0) and the Charity Cup with an emphatic 6-1 defeat of Third Lanark.

On 5 September, 1931, John Thomson was making his 211th appearance for Celtic when, after only five minutes into the second half, he was stretchered off after a collision with Sam English. Thomson never regained consciousness and died shortly afterwards in the Victoria Infirmary. Macabre as it may seem, postcards of the incident were produced soon afterwards.

Despite his name, Sam English was an Ulsterman from Coleraine. He was working at a Clyde shipyard when he attracted the attention of Rangers who spotted him scoring prolifically for Yoker Athletic. His Rangers career saw him gaining two Scottish Cup Championship medals and he was twice capped for Ireland. After the tragedy ('It was an accident' said Celt Jimmy McGrory) he soon moved to Liverpool. This portrait of the player was distributed in the 1930s by the *Topical Times*. It was part of series that came in various sizes and this one measured 9 x 24 cm.

Back row: J. Dawson, T. Gillick, T. Craig. T. Hamilton, R. McDonald, J. Fleming, G. Jenkins.
Middle row: W. Struth (Manager), J. Marshall, A. Cheyne, J. Simpson, J. Kennedy, J. Smith, J. Drysdale, R. McPhail. A. Dixon (Trainer).
Front row: R. Main, A. McAuley, D. Gray, A. Venters, D. Meiklejohn (Captain), T. Hart, G. Brown, A. Archibald, W.G. Nicholson.

The 1933-34 season saw Rangers take a clean sweep of the honours, winning the Scottish Cup, the Glasgow Cup, The Charity Cup and the League. In the final of the Scottish Cup they trounced St Mirren 5-0 with Nicholson scoring two and McPhail, Main and Smith one each.

MITCHELL'S CIGARETTES

D. GRAY
(RANGERS)

MITCHELL'S CIGARETTES

J. SMITH
(RANGERS)

MITCHELL'S CIGARETTES

D. MEIKLEJOHN
(RANGERS)

MITCHELL'S CIGARETTES

R. McPHAIL
(RANGERS)

MITCHELL'S CIGARETTES

G. BROWN (RANGERS)

THIS SURFACE IS ADHESIVE. ASK YOUR TOBACCONIST FOR THE ATTRACTIVE ALBUM (PRICE ONE PENNY) SPECIALLY PREPARED TO HOLD THE COMPLETE SERIES

SCOTTISH FOOTBALLERS
A SERIES OF 50
15
D. GRAY
(Rangers)

A model of club consistency, Dugald Gray came to Rangers from Aberdeen Mugiemoss as a Junior International in 1925. He is one of the smallest and lightest of Rangers' players, and has to make up for this with skill in the heavy position at back. He marshals an opponent into tackling position and intervenes with unerring decision. Gray, who acknowledges a great debt to "Andy" Cunningham for his mentorship, kicks a beautiful ball of low trajectory with either foot and is master of the art of heading. He plays golf, cricket and tennis with enthusiasm.

ISSUED BY
STEPHEN MITCHELL & SON
BRANCH OF THE IMPERIAL TOBACCO CO.
(OF GREAT BRITAIN & IRELAND), LTD.

Stephen Mitchell, the Glasgow cigarette manufacturer (and benefactor of the Mitchell Library) produced two sets of footballer cards, fifty in each set. The first, distributed in 1934 and called 'Scottish Footballers', included four Rangers players (these are the portrait cards here). The following year a set entitled 'Scottish Football Snaps' showing action shots was produced, although this time featuring only one Ranger player, George Brown.

THIS SURFACE IS ADHESIVE. ASK YOUR TOBACCONIST FOR THE ATTRACTIVE ALBUM (PRICE ONE PENNY) SPECIALLY PREPARED TO HOLD THE COMPLETE SERIES

SCOTTISH FOOTBALL SNAPS
A SERIES OF 50
4
G. BROWN
(Rangers)

George Brown is one of the most polished players in the Rangers team. He is Scotland's first choice for the left-half position, and he is eminently suited to this high class of football. He has played many brilliant games for the Rangers, and is essentially an attacking half-back. He makes a good left-wing support for McPhail, and often carries the ball as far forward as the penalty area. He has also played at inside forward. Rangers secured Brown in face of keen competition from Ashfield at the end of the Intermediate dispute in 1931. He is here shown just prior to the England v. Scotland match at Hampden in 1935.

ISSUED BY
STEPHEN MITCHELL & SON
BRANCH OF THE IMPERIAL TOBACCO CO.
(OF GREAT BRITAIN & IRELAND), LTD.

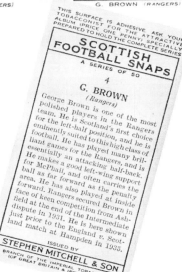

Back row: J. Dawson, J. Smith, D. Wallace, J. Simpson, J. Drysdale, W. Cheyne, R. Campbell, W. Thornton, G. Jenkins.
Middle row: W. Struth (Manager), J. Stewart, R. McPhail, J. Galloway, T. Soutar, T. McKillop, J. Reid, G. McKenzie,
J. Fiddis, J. Turnbull, R. McDonald, A. Dixon (Trainer).
Front row: J. Kennedy, D. Gray, D. McLatchie, A. Venters, T. Hart, D. Meiklejohn (Captain), R. Main, G. Brown, D. Kinnear, A. Winning, A. McAuley.

In 1936 Ardath Tobacco Co. Ltd issued a marathon set of 165 Scottish Football Teams with the Rangers card above featuring as No. 110.

One famous story from the days of cigarette cards is about a football manager who would not contemplate buying a new player unless he had been featured on a card. This was the only way he could be really sure he was buying a good footballer! Collecting cigarette cards of footballers has exploded in the last few years and it seems that demand has outstripped supply. This is a selection of pre-1940 tobacco cards.

Many boys' comics and confectioners gave away what are now referred to as 'trade cards', i.e. those not given away by tobacco firms. Most of the cards given away by comics such as the *Adventure* or *Topical Times* are quite common whereas non-comic cards are much more scarce.

The 90,000 fans who witnessed this match will never forget it. Rangers fielded Dawson, Gray, Shaw, Watkins, Young, Symon, Waddell, Gillick, Smith, Williamson and Johnstone. They were soon behind: in the third minute direct from a free kick, then Willie Waddell missed a penalty before Dynamo added a second. Shortly before half-time, Jimmy Smith pulled one back and then in the second half it was all Rangers. They equalised when George Young scored from the penalty spot. Substitutes were allowed but Dynamo took this to extremes when in the second half it was discovered that they had twelve players on the field!

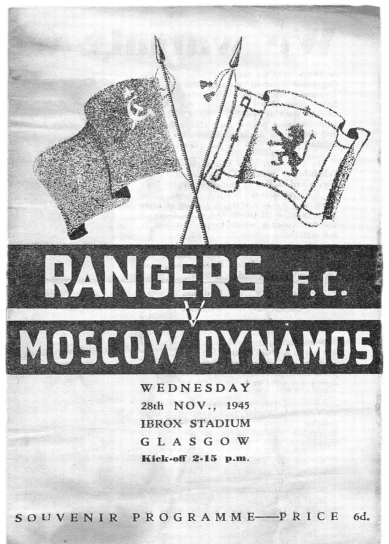

RANGERS F.C.
V
MOSCOW DYNAMOS

WEDNESDAY
28th NOV., 1945
IBROX STADIUM
GLASGOW
Kick-off 2-15 p.m.

SOUVENIR PROGRAMME——PRICE 6d.

Back row: J. Smith, W. Waddell, S. Cox, I. McColl, W. Woodburn, R. Brown, G. Young, W. Rae, W. Findlay.
Front row: W. Thornton, T. Gillick, W. Williamson, J. Shaw, J. Duncanson, E. Rutherford, W. Struth (Manager).

This plain-backed card was given out by Rangers after their Scottish Cup final win over East Fife in 1950. The 3-0 victory was fairly easy for Rangers over their young opponents. Almost immediately after kick-off Findlay scored but it wasn't until the second half that Thornton added two more. This picture from the Jack Murray collection has been autographed by Jock Shaw, the Rangers captain that day.

WADDELL

GILLICK

SPORTS FAVOURITES

No. 33

W. FINDLAY
(Inside Right)
Rangers

A Motherwell lad, he played for the local Welfare Hearts and, after four games, was signed by Junior Club, Blantyre Victoria. A month later he was in senior football, signed by Webber Lees for Albion Rovers. He possesses a fine body swerve and this, added to his intelligent play puts him in the front rank of forwards. Transferred to Rangers, April, 1947.

COPYRIGHT

A. & J. DONALDSON LTD.
69 Ingram Street, Glasgow

THORNTON

DAWSON

Issued between 1948 and 1950 by A.&J. Donaldson of Glasgow, this set of over 600 sportsmen contained footballers, boxers and speedway riders amongst others. The footballers are numbered 1-247, 360-397 and 455-460 with several numbers featuring two different portraits of the same player. The cards were often referred to as the 'Big Heads' or the 'Wee Heads'. 'The Big Heads' were a copy of number s 1-90 of the 'Wee Heads'. Donaldson also produced a set called the 'Golden Series', 64 cards with yellow borders and which it is very rare to come across.

McCOLL

RAE

BROWN

COX

WADDELL

"SMASHERS"

No. 17

WILLIE WOODBURN

Centre Half
Rangers F.C.
Born Edinburgh

Height 5ft. 11ins.
Weight 12st. 5lbs.

Joined Rangers from
secondary juvenile team Ashton. Capped for Scotland
against England 1946-47 and
Wales 1947-48.

**SPORT PHOTOS
GLASGOW**

Issued in 1950, these were stapled together in packs of six and sold by confectioners. Ninety-six Scottish football cards are in the set and they seemed to be produced in batches of 32 as the first 32 are easy to find, numbers 33 to 64 quite hard, and the last batch extremely rare.

SHAW

FINDLAY

GOVAN

RUTHERFORD

Back row: J.R. Simpson (Manager), J. Hubbard, W. McCulloch, G. Niven, W. Simpson, W. Paton, D. Grierson, J. Smith (Trainer).
Middle row:J.F. Wilson (Chairman), D. Stanners, I. McColl, W. Woodburn, W. Rae, J. Little, J. Prentice, J. Lawrence (Director).
Front row: W. Waddell, S. Cox, E. Caldow, G. Young (Captain), W. Thornton, J. Shaw.

Leaving on 8 May 1954, Rangers sailed to Montreal for their Canadian and U.S. Tour on the *Empress of Scotland*, not arriving until 14 June. It marked the end of an era because both Willie Thornton and Jock Shaw had decided to retire at the end of the tour. Nine games were played on the trip and the results saw one defeat, one draw and seven wins with 36 goals scored in the process. Many exiled Scots travelled hundreds of miles just to catch a glimpse of their heroes. When other clubs tried to sign Jock Shaw he was quoted as saying, 'I want to end my days as a Rangers player . . . I could never play for any other team.'

What a man, what a captain! The three smaller cards were produced by various issuers, while the remaining two, both in full colour, are recent creations of Jim Hossack. The postcard on the right features No. 2 in a series of 'Soccer Heroes' produced by myself while the card top left shows the reverse of card No. 1 in a set of 54 'Football Greats' issued by 'The Beautiful Game Ltd'.

Two postcards produced by Rangers in the late 1940s. Willie Thornton, born in Winchburgh, West Lothian, came to Rangers from his local junior team in 1937 and gained a reputation as a clever centre forward. First capped in the 1946-47 season, he went on to play for Scotland seven times. Woodburn, born in Edinburgh, also played for Edinburgh Ashton, Musselburgh Athletic and Queen's Park Victoria XI. He was a brilliant player but, although a gentleman off the field, he was banned 'sine die' in 1954 after his fifth sending off. The ban was lifted two years later but it was too late for him to resume his playing career. He was capped for Scotland 24 times.

Season 1956-57

Season 1957-58

D. Kichenbrand

These postcards were issued between 1956 and 1958 by the *Scottish Daily Express*. Different series were issued: 'Scottish Football Teams', an unnumbered set covering two seasons, shown above); 'Scottish Footballers', a numbered set of 34 which featured this picture of D. Kichenbrand; and 'So You Think You Know Football' a series which asked questions about the game. My thanks to the *Scottish Daily Express* for permission to reproduce these cards.

A TY.PHOO SERIES OF 24   No. 10 GLASGOW RANGERS

CUT ALONG HERE

SHEARER GREIG DAVIS RITCHIE McKINNON CALDOW
HENDERSON MILLAR McMILLAN BRAND BAXTER WILSON

FAMOUS FOOTBALL CLUBS

GLASGOW RANGERS

Scotland's legendary "Light Blues" Founded 1873. Ground: Ibrox Park, Glasgow. Colours: Royal blue shirts, white shorts. Scottish League Champions 33 times. League and Cup double 8 times European Cup-Winners' Cup Finalists 1961. In 1948–9 won the Scottish League Championship, the Scottish Cup and the League Cup.

One of soccer's greatest ever, Jim starred for Raith Rovers, Rangers, Sunderland, Notts Forest & Scotland. A superb ball player, his was a unique and marvellous talent fondly recalled by those fortunate to watch him at the height of his career. 'Slim Jim' played 34 times for Scotland and won 10 major honours with Rangers.

One of only 10 of this card produced worldwide 6/10.

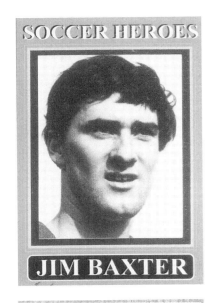

SOCCER HEROES

JIM BAXTER

GLASGOW RANGERS F.C.

JIM BAXTER
Left Half
Scotland and
Glasgow Rangers
F.C.

What a player! Anyone like myself who had the privilege of watching 'Slim Jim' in his heyday saw one of the greatest, most skilful players ever to grace the turf of Ibrox. My prize possession is a Scottish International cap, one of only five presented to him (Scottish players get one cap per season, not per game). The cards top middle and top right are the front and back of a recent Jim Hossack creation with only ten cards produced in total. However, my favourite card, bottom right, is of a smiling Jim Baxter produced by A. & B.C. Gum.

ORJAN PERRSON
RANGERS

OUTSIDE LEFT

WILLIE HENDERSON
RANGERS

OUTSIDE RIGHT

JOHN GREIG
RANGERS

CENTRE HALF

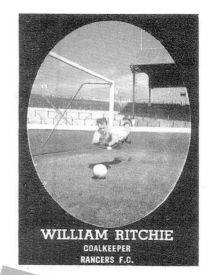

WILLIAM RITCHIE
GOALKEEPER
RANGERS F.C.

RALPH BRAND
INSIDE LEFT
RANGERS F.C.

American & British Chewing Gum Ltd, more familiarly known as A. & B.C. Gum, first produced cards in 1953. Their most popular topic was 'Footballers' with over sixty sets from 1958 to 1974 with up to 290 cards in a set. The cards of Ritchie, Miller and Brand were in the set of 81 'Footballers' in 1963. Greig, Henderson and Perrson were featured in a 1969-70 set of 42 'Footballers'. Be careful when collecting because a closer inspection of 'Orjan Perrson' should show you that it is in fact Ron McKinnon – mistakes did happen! There are many Rangers cards to collect as the company also produced many sets solely featuring Scottish players.

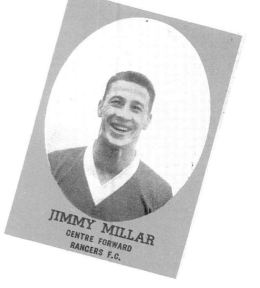

JIMMY MILLAR
CENTRE FORWARD
RANGERS F.C.

Back row: Willie Waddell (Manager), Jock Wallace (Coach), Colin Stein, Alfie Conn, Derek Johnstone, Peter McCloy, Dave Smith, Sandy Jardine, Billy Mathieson, Tom Craig (Physiotherapist).
Front row: Tommy McLean, John Greig, Alex McDonald, Willie Johnston.

The European Cup winners, 1971-72. Rangers defeated Moscow Dynamo in Barcelona on 24 May 1972 in front of 25,000 fans. The first goal was scored by Colin Stein after 24 minutes and shortly before half-time Willie Johnston added a second. In the second half Rangers increased their lead with winger Johnston getting his second of the night. Moscow Dynamo pulled two back and in spite of another pitch invasion, when the fans believed the game was over, Rangers' glory day was soon complete.

This postal cover was produced to celebrate the club's centenary and comes from the Jack Murray collection. One hundred years of great playing had passed – Oh, what I wouldn't give to have watched Allan Morton or Dave Meiklejohn! But I was fortunate enough to have seen in action Greig, Henderson, McMillan, Miller, Brand, and, to me, the greatest of them all, 'Slim Jim' Baxter. When will we see their like again?